A TUESDAY KIND OF LOVE

WRITTEN BY: LYNDSI RICHARDS
Illustrated By: Christy Johnson

ISBN: 978-1-54399-974-7

This book is dedicated to my sweet
little monkeys Makai and Rhea.
You inspire me every day!
Love - Mommy

Deep in a tropical jungle, there
lived a beautiful gorilla named
Lani. Lani loved flowers. She would
look up every morning and see
her favorite ones all the way at
the top of the trees.

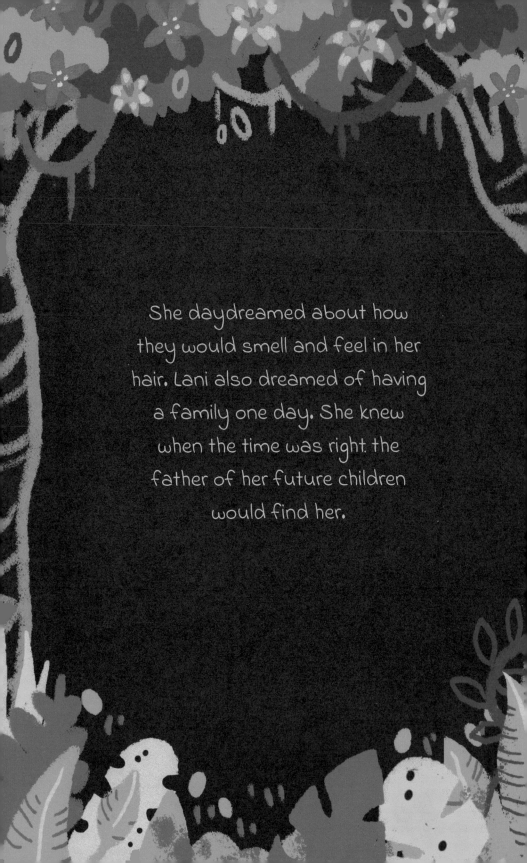

She daydreamed about how
they would smell and feel in her
hair. Lani also dreamed of having
a family one day. She knew
when the time was right, the
father of her future children
would find her.

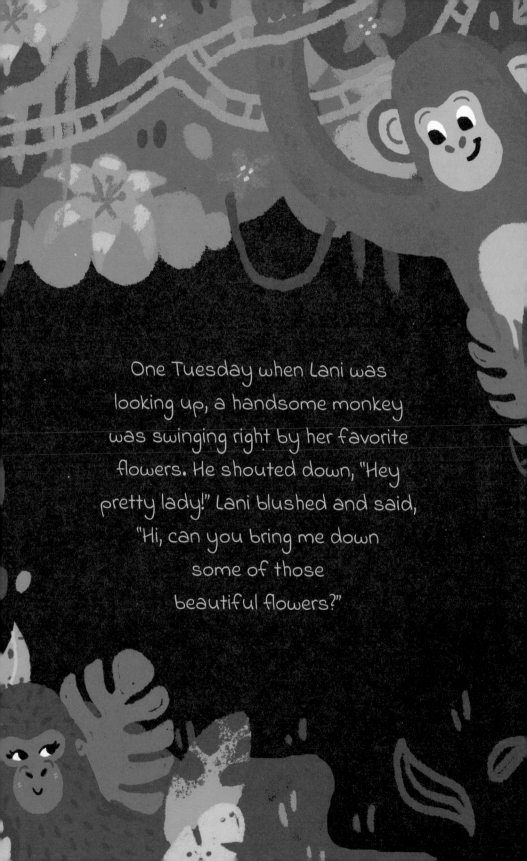

One Tuesday when Lani was
looking up, a handsome monkey
was swinging right by her favorite
flowers. He shouted down, "Hey
pretty lady!" Lani blushed and said,
"Hi, can you bring me down
some of those
beautiful flowers?"

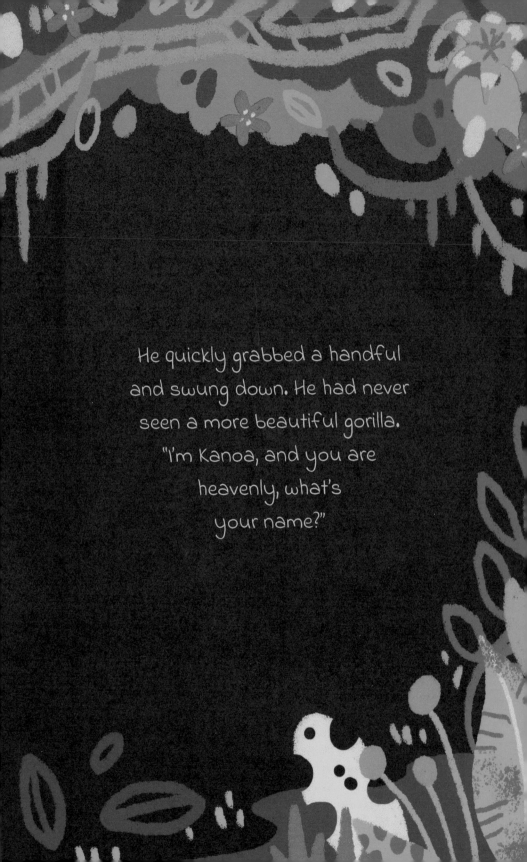

He quickly grabbed a handful
and swung down. He had never
seen a more beautiful gorilla.
"I'm Kanoa, and you are
heavenly, what's
your name?"

Lani smiled so big and said, "Why thank you, my name is Lani. You're so sweet for bringing these flowers down to me." Kanoa gave a flirty smile and then put a flower in her ear. Lani knew he was going to be someone special in her life.

Kanoa brought her flowers
every Tuesday after that.
Lani couldn't wait for
Tuesday to come, it was now
her favorite day of the week.
They would meet at the same
spot and just laugh
and play together
without a care
in the world.

They quickly fell deeply in love. Lani was so in love with him she asked Kanoa to move down to the jungle ground and make a family. She knew it was a lot for him to sacrifice because he loved his life in the trees, but Lani wasn't afraid to ask for what she really wanted.

Kanoa wanted to be with her every
minute of every day. The love Lani showed
him was like no other he had ever felt before.
He moved down from the trees
that Tuesday of course, and
now they were inseparable!

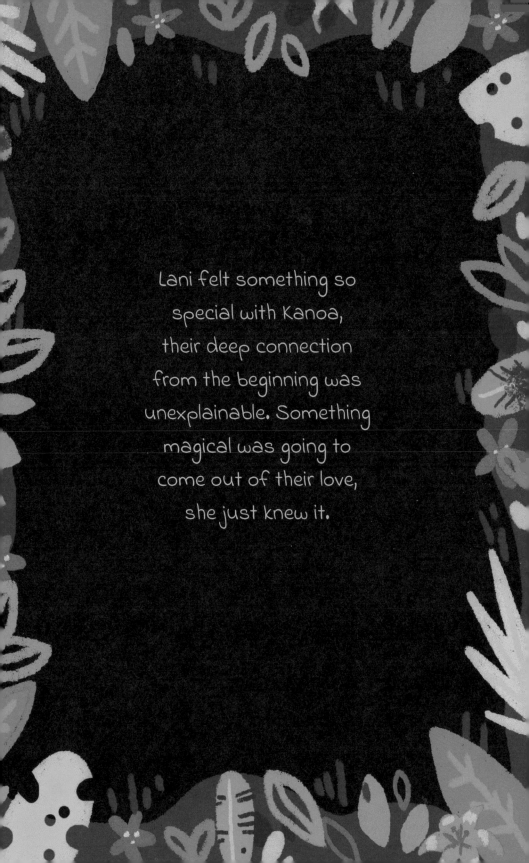

Lani felt something so
special with Kanoa,
their deep connection
from the beginning was
unexplainable. Something
magical was going to
come out of their love,
she just knew it.

A few months went by and Lani found out
she was going to have twins! A boy and a girl!
No monkey had ever made a family with a
gorilla before. The whole jungle couldn't
wait to see these babies.

Lani woke up one morning knowing today was the day her magical babies were going to be here. It was the third Tuesday of January, Lili and Koi were born! They were more perfect than anyone could ever imagine.

The first couple of months were hard on Lani, twins were not easy. Kanoa tried to help as much as he knew how to. He realized he wasn't getting the same amount of love and attention from Lani like he used to. Kanoa started to miss his old life swinging in the trees.

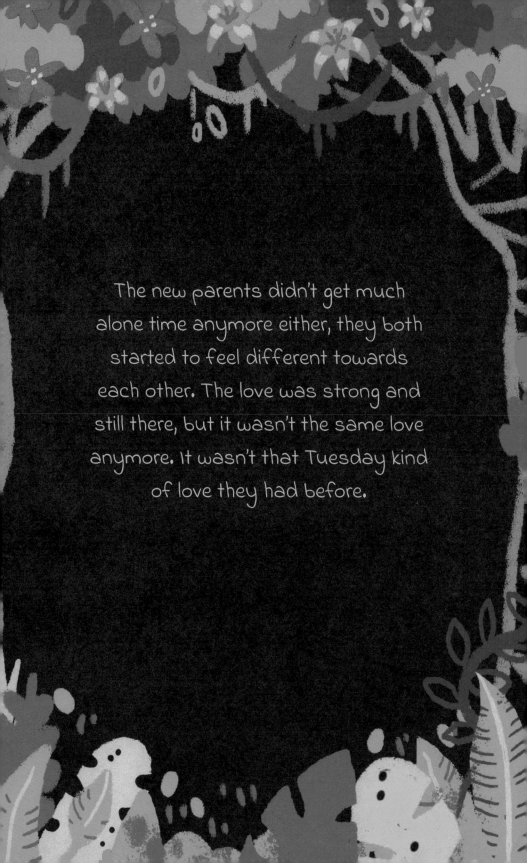

The new parents didn't get much
alone time anymore either, they both
started to feel different towards
each other. The love was strong and
still there, but it wasn't the same love
anymore. It wasn't that Tuesday kind
of love they had before.

Kanoa was sad and sometimes angry feeling like he wasn't free on the jungle ground. Lani was also feeling sad and angry. She felt like Kanoa didn't see how hard it was on her to give everyone her time and attention.

Lani felt her feelings changing for Kanoa and she noticed his pain, which made her hurt inside. He didn't know how to express how he felt, so they both just kept getting angry with each other. All they would do was argue.

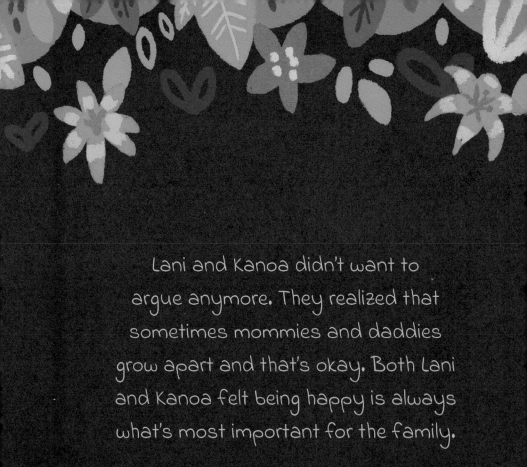

Lani and Kanoa didn't want to argue anymore. They realized that sometimes mommies and daddies grow apart and that's okay. Both Lani and Kanoa felt being happy is always what's most important for the family.

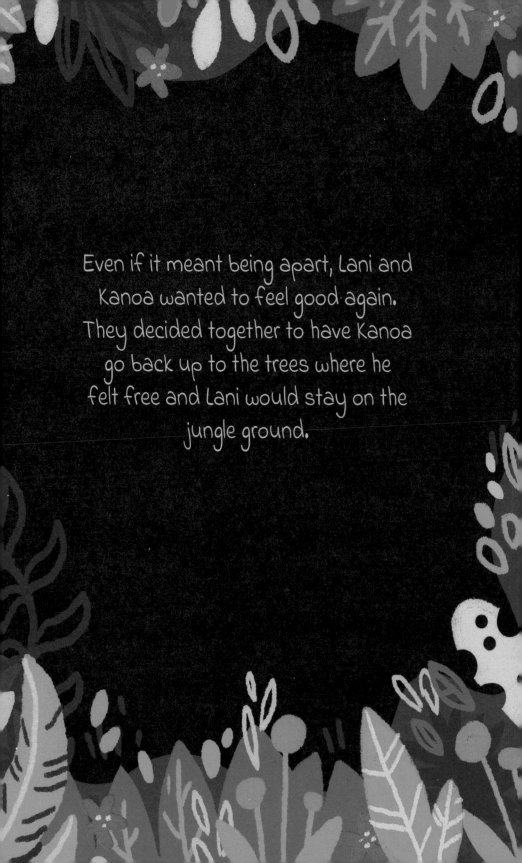

Even if it meant being apart, Lani and
Kanoa wanted to feel good again.
They decided together to have Kanoa
go back up to the trees where he
felt free and Lani would stay on the
jungle ground.

Lili and Koi would now go up with their dad every weekend and Lani started to enjoy her alone time. She saw how happy the kids were with Kanoa up in the trees. It filled her with so much joy and gratitude.

Everything was feeling right again.
Kanoa loved showing the little
monkeys how to swing up in
the trees, and Lani loved
having one on one time with
Lili and Koi on the
jungle ground.

The huge change was hard at first on all of them, but as more time went on Lili and Koi started to see the best of the jungle and the best of their parents.

Kanoa made sure every Tuesday to
swing down and bring Lani her favorites
flowers. He did this to show Lili and Koi
his appreciation and love for
their mother.

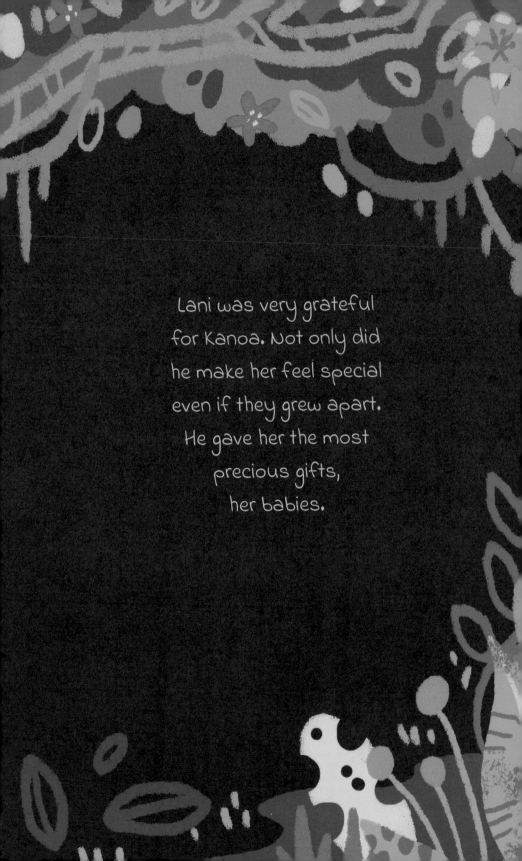

Lani was very grateful
for Kanoa. Not only did
he make her feel special
even if they grew apart.
He gave her the most
precious gifts,
her babies.

The love they shared when they
made Lili and Koi would never go
away, it was now just a little
different. The family grew stronger
and better for each other with a
new normal, it was their normal.
That Tuesday kind of love
changed a little, but it came
back into her heart.

Lani and Kanoa proved to the
jungle there is no perfect way
to love. Love is understanding,
forgiving and respectful. It can
still be powerful and pure even
if you set it free.